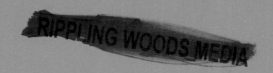

A Benjamin Blog and his Inquisitive Dog Guide

Australia

Anita Ganeri

heinemann raintree

© 2015 Heinemann Raintree
an imprint of Capstone Global Library, LLC
Chicago, Illinois

To contact Capstone Global Library, please
call 800-747-4992, or visit our web site
www.capstonepub.com

Edited by Helen Cox Cannons and Tony Wacholtz
Designed by Steve Mead
Original illustrations © Capstone Global Library
Limited 2015
Illustrated by Sernur ISIK
Picture research by Svetlana Zhurkin
Production by Helen McCreath
Originated by Capstone Global Library Limited
Printed and bound in China by CTPS

18 17 16 15 14
10 9 8 7 6 5 4 3 2 1

**Library of Congress Cataloging-in-Publication
Data**
Ganeri, Anita, 1961-
  Australia / Anita Ganeri.
       pages cm.—(Country guides, with Benjamin
Blog and his inquisitive dog)
Includes bibliographical references and index.
ISBN 978-1-4109-6846-3 (hardbound)—ISBN 978-1-
4109-6854-8 (paperback)—ISBN 978-1-4109-6869-2
(e-book) 1. Australia—Juvenile literature. I. Title.
  DU96.G363 2015
  994—dc23   2014013387

Acknowledgments
We would like to thank the following for permission
to reproduce photographs: Alamy: Jason Freeman,
16, National Geographic Image Collection, 21,
Wildlight Photo Agency, 15; Dreamstime: Joern
Schulz, 8, Ron Sumners, cover, Tamara Bauer, 6;
Getty Images: Darrian Traynor, 18, Robin Smith, 7;
iStockphotos: EdStock, 25, GCHaggisImages, 26,
Shmenny50, 10; Newscom: AFP/William West, 24,
Photoshot/World Pictures/Rick Strange, 14, Robert
Harding/Ken Gillham, 17; Shutterstock: Beata Becla,
20, Dan Breckwoldt, 13, deb22, 9, fritz16, 19, Globe
Turner, 28, Markus Gebauer, 23, Neale Cousland,
22, Qik, 12, Ralph Loesche, 4, Taras Vyshnya, 27, 29,
worldswildlifewonders, 11; XNR Productions, 5.

Some words are shown in bold, **like this.** You can find
out what they mean by looking in the glossary.

Contents

Welcome to Australia!

Hello! My name is Benjamin Blog, and this is Barko Polo, my **inquisitive** dog. (He's named after the ancient explorer **Marco Polo**.) We have just returned from our latest adventure—exploring Australia. We put this book together from some of the blog posts we wrote along the way.

Major highways

BARKO'S BLOG-TASTIC AUSTRALIA FACTS
Australia is a huge island that is also a country. It's surrounded by the Indian and Pacific Oceans. It makes up most of the **continent** of Australia, which is the smallest continent in the world.

The Story of Australia

Posted by: Ben Blog | September 5 at 9:43 a.m.

We arrived in Australia and headed straight to Tasmania, an island off the southeast coast. We're visiting the old prison at Port Arthur. This is where criminals were sent from Great Britain in the 1800s. It's surrounded by shark-infested waters, so the prisoners couldn't escape.

BARKO'S BLOG-TASTIC AUSTRALIA FACTS

In 1860, Robert Burke and William Wills led the first expedition across Australia. They died on the way back, here at Cooper Creek, from **starvation** and disease.

Rocks and Reefs

Posted by: Ben Blog | September 10 at 8:07 p.m.

From Tasmania, we headed straight into the middle of Australia to see Uluru (it used to be called Ayers Rock). It's a massive block of **sandstone** and a **sacred** place for the Indigenous Australians. We arrived here at sunset, when the rock was glowing red. What a sight!

BARKO'S BLOG-TASTIC AUSTRALIA FACTS
The Great Barrier Reef runs for 1,243 miles (more than 2,000 kilometers) along the northeast coast and is the world's biggest **coral reef**. It's home to thousands of animals—more than 1,500 types of fish, for a start.

After we left Uluru, we thought we'd explore some more of the outback. It's covered in sandy and stony deserts and is one of the hottest, driest places on Earth. I'm here in the Simpson Desert looking for Big Red, a famous **sand dune**. This work makes me thirsty!

BARKO'S BLOG-TASTIC AUSTRALIA FACTS

This amazing animal is a duck-billed platypus. It lives in rivers and streams in eastern Australia. The duck-billed platypus uses its webbed feet for swimming. It scoops up worms and shellfish from the muddy riverbed with its leathery, duck-like bill.

City Sights

Posted by: Ben Blog | September 28 at 9:59 a.m.

Most Australians live in cities around the coast. Our next stop was Sydney, the biggest city in Australia. It's home to 4.5 million people and is a busy, lively place. Barko took this snapshot of me outside the Sydney Opera House, one of the most famous landmarks in the city.

BARKO'S BLOG-TASTIC AUSTRALIA FACTS

Canberra is the capital city of Australia. It was built from scratch in 1913. This is Parliament House, where the Australian government meets. It was built in the shape of a **boomerang**.

G'day!

Many Australians have **ancestors** from Great Britain and Europe. Many others have moved to Australia from New Zealand, China, India, Italy, and Vietnam. The people in this photo are Indigenous Australians. They were the first people to live in Australia around 50,000 years ago.

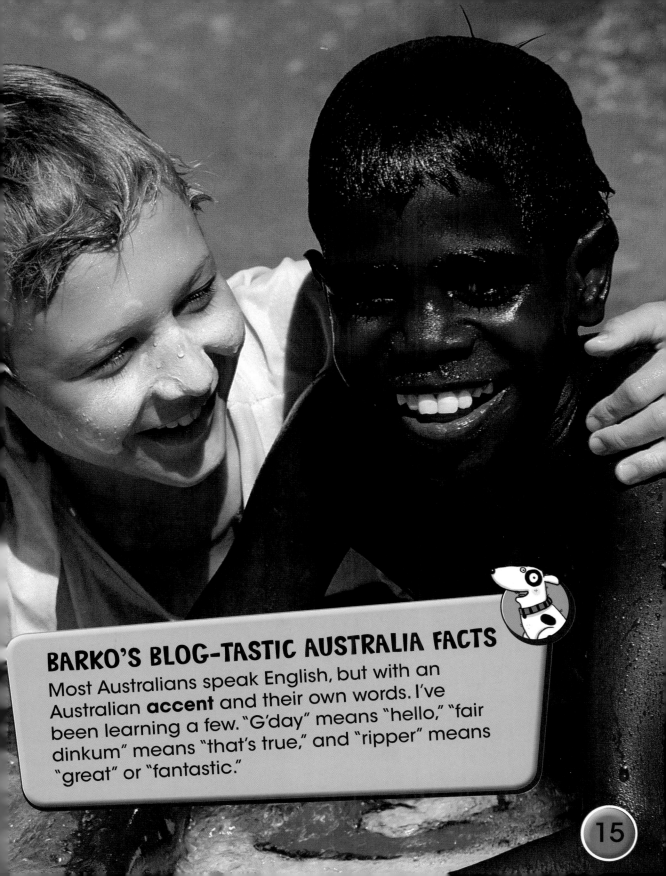

BARKO'S BLOG-TASTIC AUSTRALIA FACTS

Most Australians speak English, but with an Australian **accent** and their own words. I've been learning a few. "G'day" means "hello," "fair dinkum" means "that's true," and "ripper" means "great" or "fantastic."

In Australia, the school day usually lasts from 9 a.m. until 3:30 p.m. Most children wear uniforms and need sun hats and sunblock all summer. Some children who live deep in the Australian outback cannot get to school. They have to take their classes by radio or online instead.

BARKO'S BLOG-TASTIC AUSTRALIA FACTS

People in the Australian outback often live a long way from a hospital, so they call a flying doctor instead. The Royal Flying Doctor Service has around 60 planes and flies thousands of miles every day.

We're in the city of Melbourne for Australia Day. It's when Australians remember the arrival of the first ships from England. People are cheering and waving Australian flags as they wait for the parade to pass. Later, there's going to be a spectacular fireworks display in Docklands.

BARKO'S BLOG-TASTIC AUSTRALIA FACTS

The Indigenous Australians believe in a time called the Dreaming when their **ancestors** made the world. They remember this time with dance and music. This man is playing a traditional Indigenous Australian instrument called the **didgeridoo**.

Time for a "Barbie"

Posted by: Ben Blog | January 26 at 6:14 p.m.

It had been a long day and we were hungry, so we headed down to the beach for a barbie (barbecue). Barko couldn't wait to sink his teeth into some juicy snags (hot dogs). I stuck to shrimp and a hamburger, with **pavlova** for dessert.

BARKO'S BLOG-TASTIC AUSTRALIA FACTS

Bush tucker is food found in the wild. The Indigenous Australians in the outback lived off it for thousands of years. Would you like to dig into goanna (lizard), honey ants, or witchetty grubs? They're all on the bush tucker menu.

Crazy for Sports

Posted by: Ben Blog | March 15 at 2:30 p.m.

Staying in Melbourne, we've come to watch a game of Australian (Aussie) rules football. It is like a blend of soccer and football. Players can kick, punch, or pick up the ball, but throwing is not allowed. We're cheering for Hawthorn—one of Melbourne's top teams.

BARKO'S BLOG-TASTIC AUSTRALIA FACTS
Many Australians live near the ocean, so swimming and surfing are very popular. There are great surfing beaches around the country, like this one at Bells Beach. Surf's up, so I'm heading in.

From Cattle Stations to Opal Mines

Posted by: Ben Blog | March 19 at 7:53 a.m.

From Melbourne, we made our way west to the state of South Australia. We're spending a few days at Anna Creek cattle station, training to be jackaroos (cowboys). They have around 17,000 cattle here. We'll be using trail bikes to round them up. Yikes!

BARKO'S BLOG-TASTIC AUSTRALIA FACTS

Shimmering gemstones called opals are one of Australia's most precious **natural resources**. They're mined here in Coober Pedy, a town in the Australian outback. It gets so hot in Coober Pedy that many people have also dug themselves homes underground.

25

And Finally...

The last stop on our tour was beautiful Rottnest Island, off the coast of Western Australia. I wanted to see some quokkas. They are small, furry animals about the size of cats. Quokkas are **marsupials**, like kangaroos and wallabies, and are very rare. Here's a photo I took.

I am here!

BARKO'S BLOG-TASTIC AUSTRALIA FACTS

This is Sydney Harbor Bridge. It's nicknamed "the coat hanger" because of its arch shape. You can climb to the top for a breathtaking view of the city, but you can't be afraid of heights.

Australia Fact File

Area: 2,969,907 square miles
(7,692,024 square kilometers)

Population: 23,371,900 (2014)

Capital city: Canberra

Other main cities: Sydney, Melbourne, Brisbane

Language: English

Main religion: Christianity

Highest mountain: Mount Kosciuszko
   (7,310 feet/2,228 meters)

Longest river: Murray River
   (1,558 miles/2,508 kilometers)

Currency: Australian dollar

Australia Quiz

Find out how much you know about Australia with our quick quiz.

1. What is Uluru made from?
a) opals
b) limestone
c) **sandstone**

2. What does "ripper" mean?
a) great
b) awful
c) sunny

3. What is a **didgeridoo**?
a) an Australian drink
b) an Australian animal
c) an Australian musical instrument

4. What sport does Hawthorn play?
a) baseball
b) Aussie rules football
c) basketball

5. What is this?

Answers
1. c
2. a
3. c
4. b
5. Sydney Harbor Bridge

Glossary

accent way of speaking and pronouncing words

ancestor relative from the past

boomerang wooden, V-shaped object that was thrown for hunting

continent one of seven huge areas of land on Earth

coral reef long structure made from coral that grows along the coast

didgeridoo long, pipe-like musical instrument

inquisitive interested in learning about the world

Marco Polo explorer who lived from about 1254 to 1324. He traveled from Italy to China.

marsupial mammal with a pouch in which its babies grow

natural resource natural material that we use, such as coal, oil, or wood

pavlova dessert made from meringue, topped with fruit and cream

sacred another word for being holy, or special, as part of a person's religion or beliefs

sand dune giant heap of sand found in deserts and on beaches, piled up by the wind

sandstone soft rock that can be red, brown, or gray

starvation death caused by lack of food

Find Out More

Books

Colson, Mary. *Australia* (Countries Around the World). Chicago: Heinemann Library, 2012.

McCollum, Sean. *Australia* (Country Explorers). Minneapolis: Lerner, 2008.

Ward, Chris. *Discover Australia* (Discover Countries). New York: PowerKids, 2012.

Web sites

Facthound offers a safe, fun way to find Internet sites related to this book. All of the sites on Facthound have been researched by our staff.

Here's all you do:

Visit *www.facthound.com*

Type in this code: 9781410968463

Index